these things i crave

Also by Lucky:

Water Media
Violent Words for Beautiful People
O.G. Indigo
Inside Dark Light

Contact: sakulryder@gmail.com

Portrait by Krista Nicole

These Things I Crave
©2006 Lucky Ryder

ISBN 978-1-7774688-5-9

All rights reserved.

No part of this publication may be reproduced, distributed or transmitted in any form or by any means, electronic, mechanical, photocopying, recording or otherwise, without the prior written permission of the author.

These Things I Crave

by
Lucky Ryder

(An autobiography in
Attention Deficit Disorder
friendly fragments)

CONTENTS

11	WILLOW
12	THERE ARE NO BONES IN MY HANDS BUT I STILL LOOKED GREAT IN VOGUE
14	ST. ANDREW'S CROSS
15	PILLARS
19	SIPHONING COLOR FROM THE ECHOES
20	JAUNDICE
21	SUGAR
22	CUT THE THROAT OF A LAMB IT WILL SURELY SEE STARS DASHED TO PIECES IN THE CHERRYWOOD CRAWLSPACE
23	THE SOUND I MAKE WHILE FREEFALLING TOWARD YOU
24	TERROR AND CALM: THE WIDDENSHIN FOOTBLADES
28	THE SHELTER INSIDE MYSELF
29	CIRCLE PIT, WITH LOVE
30	CONVECTION TOWER REMIX
31	GREASE MONKEY REMIX
32	COAL TRAIN REMIX
33	SOCK PUPPET REMIX
34	BLIGHTER REMIX
35	INFRASONIC
36	DEATH BY PLANE
37	BRIGHT EYES
39	DAISIES
40	3,200 DEGREES

42	AND ALL AT ONCE, SILENCED
43	WHEN ROSES CUT OUR HANDS OPEN TO RELEASE THE BURNING LIGHT
44	HORSES
45	ROOT
46	EMPTY BOXES IN EMPTY ATTICS
49	SPARKS FROM YOUR MOUTH AND STONES FROM YOUR SHOULDERS
53	BLUE JAY
54	CORTICAL MIDLINE STRUCTURES
55	PARACHUTES
57	BAAL AND THE MILKMAN'S WIFE
58	THE TAKING
59	UNTITLED PART II
61	THE FALLING
62	NOISE NOISE NOISE
63	OIL
64	WHEN WE WERE CHILDREN
65	WHALES
66	THE BACK WALL
67	FAMILY PORTRAIT
68	FALTAENIA
73	POSTMORTEM
74	TAROT

A NOTE ON AUDIO IMBEDDING

Recordings of the following instruments have been electronically and graphically imbedded at key points into the pages of this book for dramatic and artistic purposes: harpsichord, electrical and acoustic one, six, and twelve string guitars, acoustic bass guitar, brass and silver trumpets, djembe, bodhran, Roland TR-808, violins and violas, cello, keyboards, circuit bent speak and math, trash cans, various sampling devices, fog, jaw harp, wind tunnels, vocal effect pedals, toy piano, the Eighth Stalactite Bell Ensemble, crystal glasses, dog and train whistles, rotary telephones, feedback generator, theremin, waterphone, turntables, ceramic dishes, pipe and glass organ.

The smoking of fags, spliffs, old negatives, ground flash bulbs, dmt, cloves, skeleton keys, lsa, book binding glue, fresh sulfur, twelve-inch pipes constructed of ancient purple heart wood and packed with dried lavender, fine Italian suits, Honduran cigars, Beatles LPs, brown sugar, skin grafts, and white picket fences is greatly encouraged.

WILLOW

We fade like shutters
placed in hillsides.
Thin frost marks of trees
skew the sight of us,
only slightly.

We appear and disappear
like your breath in the cold.
The vapor
presses against us
like mighty gentle palms,
leaving wet marks in the grass.
Evaporating more,
every time you inhale
and once we're gone;
you remember.

When knee deep in the snow
how we felt like new leaves.
How when you
pressed us in books
along with the lilies,
and foxglove.
The pages absorbed our moisture,
and still our bodies
                        only got heavier.

THERE ARE NO BONES IN MY HANDS BUT I STILL LOOKED GREAT IN VOGUE

While attending the opera,
there is a woman dressed in green fur
sipping absinthe from a golden glass flask
in the seat to your right.

The smell of wormwood
is traipsing across your tongue,
up the back of your throat
and has taken residence
in the mixed media of your nostrils.

You offer her Pez.

She casually accepts,
scuffing her moccasins across
the checkered soda shoppe floor.

"If your hands are sewn together..."
She begins.

Leaning in to your shoulder
her faceted emerald lips pivot
from lapel towards your ear
and whisper amidst the mutual
hallucinations of one other.

"...Don't be ashamed when you are
the only one not clapping.

You are tall and distinguished
in your pin stripe suit.
The ribbon is frayed, but the crowd
is just cymbals and deep breaths
in balloons filled with nitrous.

If your lungs begin to freeze,
worry not.

I will replace your heart
with this flask.

I speak from experience,
the poison will warm your bones."

ST. ANDREW'S CROSS

The veins in my arms shattered like catastrophe inkwells
laid siege to by finger painting novelists
bent on scribing my story, on the walls of my castle.

Fires lit on hilltops
and drums sounding
in the distance.

Oak cannons shifted twelve degrees east
and archers held at steady.

I am a king without arms,
but not a ruler without tools.

PILLARS

She had been told at once this visage just did not cut the cloth, and how no courtesan could curtail his love for her. The walls between them had grown too thin to be that glass between hands, the cellophane between lips, and even years ago, too thin to be the satin that pressed between their hips.

Tandem meditation, bespoke, encapsulated and dosed in the glinting twilight. Sequins flared under the porcupine's hide. The quills coiled red wood banister around their arms, finding foundation slowly at the base of their spines. Prisoners in the wide walled glass house they built for themselves. Shard by shard from the days spent lapping wine from copper plates in the lowest rooms where the furnaces fused with bedrock.

Untamed rose bushes flourish,
encroaching deeply and without shame.

Plots of land once vacant
now surrounded by colors
unlike color.

Radiating visuals reminiscent
of nothing known, nothing nostalgic.
Anything to swoon the rain

the way they used to swoon.
Filling entire rooms
with their only passion
sprung from their only pain.

Fruitless trees wrought from the ground, giving way
to young bright blossoms spilling forth like smoke.
Oranges, crimsons, yellows wafting and curling dreams
that simply change direction and shape when she swung
her sword through them.

Weapons in sport.
Scents spun verbatim.

Death plunges in solitude
forged long ago twist and crack
and with such relief
lifted loftily from the sheath.
Fingers rested on the hilt
so softly did she
furrow against the sounds
of the dry leaves and liquid steel sting.

Whole handedly, where fingers met.
The narrow edge of their bodies
thirsted heavily from where they did not.
Palms up, and dilating.

From the eye's inner cradle, the bellows sung deep.
Quizzically rested nimbly upon the knot of his necktie.
A sweaty dew streaking the lump in his
quivering stone throat.

Bound like a crystal sphere's cat-like dew drop
dribbling upon the tip of the blade.

Reverberation echoing parallel to the mossy forest floor
stretching the breadth of city roof tops.
She made haste and beckoned the storming winds.
Arching from crown to crown.
Tongue to tongue.
Lifting her from his paths of green
to her own galleon of budding slopes.
Sliver slipping bloodline
from chin to forehead,
smoldering shadowy glaciers
in light of the dawn's own pistols
and careening upon one another.

Gunmetal to grain and burl,
and cannons over canyons.

Their battleship's figureheads
forged in forest fires. Breaking bows
insurgent as pavement driving upwards
from the stomach of the earth and droning on.

Colossal broadswords against storefronts.
Churning parks and walkways into
hemorrhaging riptides and cursing waves.
Unseen bodies tossed from doorsteps
out into the fog and then lost.

Together, lock jawed and swirling.
Cascading infernos high above the metro,
pouring into one another's bodies
like a flood of flames from the sky.
Turning roses and mosses
into icicles and frost
and her arctic into a blizzard
where every snowflake has a different name,
and his forest, into a bed of coals
where buried and forgotten seeds
wake to devour the warmth.

But there are handprints on the doors,
and the copper has gone dry,
and a young and thirsty wind is filling the room.

SIPHONING COLOR FROM THE ECHOES

Her tongue,
cotton candy pink
behind white teeth.

When her ruby lips parted
she exhumed sounds
I've never heard before.

Her vibrancy wavered me
until I was on my knees.

She never once spoke.

But it was her voice that made
these gray tears turn blue.

JAUNDICE

(When I can no longer see the skin on me
I'll know the fur has over grown my hands.)

Delving new perception
pulls my chest to new dimensions
and my lungs to fill themselves,
from orb to omelet
and my skin
to curry yellow once again.

SUGAR

I kiss gravel and purse my lips
against the white walls around me.
These were just my limbs
while I was sleeping.
Strewn tightly across the bedframe.
Ships sails set the sea
between my nose and toes,
the back of my tongue and teeth.

Where I hear the itch, I scratch.
Oppose the plexiglass of my eyes
clothed in static and my iris swords
dulled by rusting sheets.

It hurt much worse still, just like before
stemming outside from in.

I clawed at the windows
while pushing hard against the brick
until in my dreams I was eyeless.
I medicated myself with the virus
and if I had a tongue still
or a brain to move it.

Well, I'd tell you the difference
between being well and sick.

CUT THE THROAT OF A LAMB AND IT WILL SURELY SEE STARS DASHED TO PIECES IN THE CHERRY WOOD CRAWL SPACE

Oxygen masks and stars
and knives are all you need
once the body's in place.

Give it a name,
give it a face,
and all the rest
will fall into space.

THE SOUND I MAKE WHILE FREE FALLING TOWARDS YOU

Maybe I will be poignant and decipher
the secrets in text stitched along
the elastic around your underwear.
Cupping those moisturized,
silk stretchmark hips that you wear
with such a sauntering comfort,
in your left, right, c-train waltz.
Sneaky glimpses of sun kissed waist line
between small holes in 'em t-shirts,
and the leather belt holding up your cut off fatigues.

Fresh bouquets at your sides lending a hand
to the Gerber daisy accents of your eyes.
An unlanguishing persona.
A flowering complex that taps petal toes
under and over rubber soles.
Warm underground behind wooden doors.

Blue smoke swirling hazily
in the basement light.
You question me inquisitively
like tongue spinning poi,
and every time, I am wordless
as a viola in vibrato.
Lost to decipher your code.

TERROR AND CALM:
THE WIDDERSHIN FOOT BLADES

All witnesses eventually die
(due to the condemnation of light),
all witnesses eventually die.

While the accident that keeps you warm inside
is slowly dropping clips from the film,
from the reel, color from the slide.
Filling the room with black perfume.
Dazzling away from the melting box.
This, crucible.
This, melting pot.

Capsizing projection, destroy the evidence.
Smash the urns, smoke my ashes and speak to me.
Confess to me for I am in the walls of leaves,
tinkering through your bones
like through metal shafts.
I am in the knobs you fuck with keys.
I can see the sugar swimming through
the veins of your heaving engine.
You can taste me in your forked tongue
whisking through the breeze,
in the apples and cooked meat you eat
I am there, picking under your sleeves.

You leave the knives closeted.
Boxed in pale widows.
Radio static clapped on their ears
and bleeding temples.

Their heads packed with stale air
and decay in the wiring.
Splattering electricity through the garden
sworn to uphold the snake head detection.
Detox for the victims.
Shoving through grates of fish wire
guaranteed to not be basted to the sheets.
Dropping like hail through the gates.
Cutting cobra consensus clued in too late.

I commence the slash down of that too
to the tune of gaping mouths gumming
away at the wood rot and evidence.
Under the pretense of out of sight
therefore victimless.

Steadfast.
I am doused in terror and calm.
I see right through you and
your attempt to dilute the harm.
Let me trade your limbs for aspen.
Your muscles for coal.
Baptize in my venom

until your hands and face are holes.
My talons in your jaw bone.
Emblazon your femurs to my throne.
I swath you in drab linen
and crush you under stone.

This is not the accident
that will keep you warm.

I am conducting a plan
and devising a bomb.
I am doused in starry
terror and calm.

I will sleep tonight,
and purge out in my dreams.

Is sleepwalking sleep walking when
there are no footprints behind me?
Is sleepwalking sleep walking when
there are no footprints that I can see?

The blood-soaked sheets
wrapped around the fired aspen bedpost,
dripping out of the yawning window.

That was my way out of here.
This is my vein out of this place

and I swear I am outside the walls
before I even breach the gates.

I'm having my veins drawn out
through my arms.
I emerge from blood-soaked sheets
and the window that yawns.

I am almost.

I am almost that ghost
with the blood on his feet.
Sleep walking is only sleep walking
when you have somewhere to be.

I am almost.

I am almost that ghost
with the blood on his feet.

You were not sleepwalking.
Those are my footprints you see.

THE SHELTER INSIDE MYSELF

You are my angel
rocking back and forth,
deep within my jaw of glass.
Powdered bones shifting
upon the black and white keys.

I listen to you play.
Breathing and lissome.

You feed me silver wine and golden thread.

Your wings fold around me
and I am sheltered from
the twirling dervish.

Harpsichord notes
resounding through the tension.
Uncountable moments,
paused in suspension.

I listen to you play
and do not attempt to speak.

Sifting calmly.
Calmly sifting,
in among the piano keys.

CIRCLE PIT, WITH LOVE

You have been with me the longest.
Since I needed someone
who wasn't there, you were.
You were the growing inside me, secret.
Until you were ready to come out, prepared.

You were the shitkicker, the disturber,
the fighter, the survivor.

With your scraped and skinny limbs,
torn Chuck Taylors, chapped lips,
and brass knuckles.

You were always the first to throw
a punch, and the last to kiss back.
Though you always did.

Thank you for your short words and tough love.

Every time I crash the pit at a show
I know you're there beside me.
Your Chucks in the dust
and knuckles in the air.
Screaming out and letting go.

CONVECTION TOWER REMIX

Humming birds carry
fleeting expressions.

Spilling pollen,
blood sugar.

Honey stung/stuck spiny cornstalk.

Scorching roads of flour
thread whole wheat.

Crop circles sweeter
with every sighting.

GREASE MONKEY REMIX

Robot hearts slide into pieces
like rusted bolts
blown towards ocean's tide.

Molecules of no man's land.

Separating wet suit
from dry dock.

COAL TRAIN REMIX

Inkwells upturned,
wrapped in red cedar floors.

My droogs and I out of order.

You flounder
perplexed.

We have beseeched
outer cobblestone
opposite the threshold.

There are no good byes,
and we have not the time
to apologize.

SOCK PUPPET REMIX

I am longing for my twin
lost to dryer ambience.

Hot air crag stabs.
Death by Narnia.

We were Siamese foot jackets
separated at birth.

If there is no reunion soon
I will unravel.

Singing thread.
A flaming sweater's soul.

BLIGHTER REMIX

Interruptions instigate
insinuated slivers of sound.

Battering what else is to be heard.

A nothing second.
Less than invention.
Surpassing introduction.
Bathing off without conclusion
yet shaking the tresses all the same.

My arms
and
...
your feet.

Silence can be an answer too.

INFRASONIC

Cleaving leaves will
bring the trees on me
and shooting stars
will not to say.

The smooth bass strokes
convey the clouds in me.

'Listen'
I can hear the cymbals say.

Over the speakers.
Dripping
under your feet.

That love will tear us apart,
and respectively fade away.

DEATH BY PLANE

I will never look at you the same since
you dipped your nose toward the ground.

Tipping your wings
to thread through the clouds.

At twenty thousand feet
the no smoking light goes out,
and I light up for the last time.

Neon orange cherries breathing
in the dust filled dawn.

Ventriloquists dancing
to shattered turbine songs.

If you ever see me again,
I will be wrapped
in shrouds of sheet metal.
The wreckage, sustained.
I am asleep
in the under carriage.

Dummies lost
to death by plane.

BRIGHT EYES

We were as ravenous as wolves.

Filling our mouths
with each other's tails
and eating all we could
until my throat was yours
and yours was mine,
and our bones were showing
and gleaming white.

Laughter rained up from the soil,
drenching our remains.

These sounds were the first
to ever touch the snow.
Up the spines of willows
and flaring through the updrafts
into the dark and blue.
Splattering the sky
with bright eyes and ears,
and hands, and feet
to transcend the heavens
and the earth.

Creating newborn infants
and hearts to fill them.

This was the beginning of man,
and such ways will be the end.

When the stars
will remove our hearts.

The trees
will remove the stars,

and we will be returned
to the wolves.

Teeming and ravenous once again.

DAISIES

I
met a girl
with her head
in a bowl.

Puking up
And choking
cuz the booze
went to her brain.

As she did
she said that
she loves God.

Hallelujah.

Amen.

3,200 DEGREES

The stars in the sea
wash out with the tide.

My feet are dry in the sand
and I cannot see the waves.

When a starfish dies
it's browning limbs curl like ribbon.

Drying stone sharp and brittle.
Collapsing under the salt in the air.

A cluster of ocean glass
in the palm of my hand.

As the sun ages
it will swell into a red giant,
lifting me out towards the waves.

White noise will fill my ears.
Water droplets will tear against
my body and I will swear I am coming.

I will drain myself.
Replacing the blood in my veins
with the Sun's rushing breath.

The glass star in my hands
will explode into white light.

Deafening my ears
and blinding my eyes.

And I will know that I am home,

finally.

AND ALL AT ONCE, SILENCED

Static light saturates wet skin.
Hot drapes burn midnight oil.

Lamplighters exploding
quietly along the roads.

Irises opened wide and mouths gapping.

Soft light flashes into the room
as we sleep like children aloft
in the woods and rivers.

Shock wave. Still frame. Plate glass.
Decimate. Headlights. Dirt roads.
Last call. Water front. Fishing boat.
Breath held. Skin ripples.

A wall of sound.

Hira drums in irrigation channels.
A burning bodhran
in the midnight moon.

WHEN ROSES CUT OUR HANDS OPEN TO RELEASE THE BURNING LIGHT

At night the disco god
is hard pressed between the slats.
He is in amongst the turnstiles
where he is screwing himself into a wheel.

His tongue is wide like a shovel,
slathered and swollen,
filling the space in his head
and banded tight.

Corsets and chastity belts
for his voice box and lungs.
He is the bitter blood
between my thighs.
He is the arsenic in my hair.
He is the poison between my eyes.
He is the ash in my mouth
and the boils on my body.
He is a defect I have grown to love.

My disco god has his
tongue in the gears.
But he feels with his hands
and he is building a bomb.

HORSES

Post confession fishing line
stitches closed wounds
once known to be
the crypt of royal teeth.

Gold and dust folded in between
heavy drapes of flesh.
A cabaret, a bouillabaisse,
concoctions spilling over the river's width.

The boiling point of a cathedral's bells.

Steamy fairy tales leading hopeful women
to a shining castle with no knight.

ROOT

Lapping up ice
to bury my feet in the snow
and tie my hands to the trees,
I find trampled flowers
and shattered branches.

Folded in half and held still by time.

Elegant desolation.
Beautiful destruction.

I am fading like a freezing iris.
I am stretching like winter nights.
I am wilting like an elder bloom.

Icicles on bird's wings,
ceasing day time flights.

EMPTY BOXES IN EMPTY ATTICS

And we write poems
about tiny nothings.

Fleeting moments.

Hopes, dreams,
childhood wishes
that seem to vent off
under our office doors.

Across the street
and out of the city
where they become lost
under dry thickets and
old farm house wood.

In empty fields and
in barns that have
long since fallen
into disuse.

In haylofts where stray cats gave birth.
Abandoning their newborns
in the darkest and safest corners.

How long before they grew still?

Before their time too short
to have ever begun, folded
in around them so tightly
it pressed the space from
their bodies and the eyes
from their sockets.
Cradled in the crumbling hay.
Grown brittle from the dry heat.

On weekend trips outside the city
we find more reminders of mothers
no longer to be found.
We are reminded of when they went,
and how we will follow.

Old nylons caught in the wind on rusting nails
like the transparent tissue paper skin
we fear we'll grow in later days.

When the last of our blue, blue blood will drip
through our veins, wavering against the fuzz
of flannel sheets in cozy retirement homes.

Breakfast with friends.
Lunch at one.
Cribbage and backgammon to follow.
Paper cups and heart meds.
Watching the squirrels.

Sharing old stories
we've told so many times.
Paintings of people in row boats.
We imagine they're going
somewhere we have been
while we write letters,
some of the last we will pen.

Recalling the moments
that made us whole
and brought us home,
and give us peace
in the beds we now lay.

While some moments,
we thought of
for the last time
so long ago.

Tiny nothings,
hopes, dreams,
childhood wishes now
lost in the sunken eyes
Of those empty shell kittens.
Too precious to care for
and too long ago to keep.

SPARKS FROM YOUR MOUTH
AND STONES FROM YOUR SHOULDERS

My reflection burns deep
in the melting glass
of the oven door.
The spoons inside
glowing roman candle red
dissolve a potion to ignite my wings.

When the guests arrive
I'll drink it down,
stringy glass and steel.

I will smolder through
the pile of coats on the bed
and tearing through the ceiling
I will rush away from here screaming

'I am coming home to you.
I am coming home,
you heroine of twelve packs and lace,
stringy glass and chrome.'

You will be so relaxed
to know that I am coming home.

And when you hear me in the distance

you will drop glass bowls.
You will streak out of the house
wearing an old t-shirt of mine.

You will run until all
of the color is left behind you.
Until you are black and white
like Charlie Chaplin
or Marilyn Monroe.

And seizing up on the side of the
New Jersey turnpike you will crumble.

You will bare your teeth
and gnaw at the stones
that seep from your shoulders.

You know when I arrive that
I will be high and incoherent.
That I will stop at nothing
until I take you with me.
We'll drive so, so far away
with the top down.
The wind cutting into our teeth
like knives sending sparks
echoing
in the midnight noise.

Trailing behind the headlights
the glow of our eyes
sprawling out behind us
like silk scarves
that pull at our hair.
Pushing us into static.
Jumping like bad reception
along these narrow dirt roads.

You will lean over in your seat
and hold me until your skin
becomes gray with soot,
and your lungs fill with
the ash from my mouth.

Your tongue will melt
against the words
lost in the rushing air
as you tell me your name,
and other trivialities
that swim from your lips
becoming distant
wavering nuances
on the way to my ear.

You'll ask me questions about myself.
About who I am and who I've been with.

You will whisper,
'Where are you taking me?'

I will just smile as the brakes compress.
Crushing glass and sending us
shredding through silence.
Our torn coat tails in flames,
lethargically burning
pretty, dirty words,
across the stars and their sky.

BLUE JAY

Little bird when you beat your wings
until you fall from your nest
and lay wilting in the grass,
under drowning rain,
above nothing comforting
with nothing left to do.

Smile brightly to spite gravity,
and never regret the things
others said you could never do.

CORTICAL MIDLINE STRUCTURES

All these people are wholly

      holy skinned,
and completely skinned is
    what they are.

PARACHUTES

Your parachutes
never held
you up before.

As it is
you'll never ask
for the wind
again.

I guess they
never told you
your worth...

As it is
it never got
this cold
before

with the wind cutting
deep into your
eyes.

The lines shaking
so loudly
like lightening.

They all never
held you so close
before.

As it was
when you
were in the air

they would do all they could
to pull your parachute
to the ground.

BAAL AND THE MILKMAN'S WIFE

The skulls of bulls
make excellent masks
for when we stand tall
and bury our hands in the sand
we pretend to see god
through wide and empty eyes
that were never our own.

THE TAKING

Your daughters will bare themselves.
Stretched out on butcher paper
under gleaming lights.

Scissors and thread.

Lips pulled taut.
Thighs shimmer with disinfectant.

Poison in the great halls.

When zippers are applied,
pressure is easily released.

UNTITLED PART II

When your train stops coming
I'll sell everything I own.

I'll rent out a one room flat downtown
and paint the walls purple.

I'll shave my head
and let the rain leak down
through the ceiling,
where posters of Kurt Cobain
and Sid Vicious will fade
and curl at the edges.

The bathroom bare
and stained
will smell of tobacco,
a hint of the iron taste
of blood in the air.

In the mirror's reflection
all that looks back at me
is a grainy frame from a film
that was stopped at precisely
the wrong moment.

I stand there waiting for what I see to change.

But it doesn't,
and I remember

I am out of cigarettes.

I can almost feel you,
even here, right now.

Your long thin hands around my arm
and your breath against my cheek.

I can almost hear your voice.

THE FALLING

People like me know no one.
We thread ourselves into glass cocoons
and drag our useless bellies
beneath the machines and across the concrete.

We take to the dirt and
stay away from the lights.
Weaving epiphanies out of roots
we know by touch alone and digging deeper.
Always deeper to escape the sound.
If we never breathed fresh air again,
it would be too soon.

Falling and falling far beneath the ground
we live off of our waste and feel born again.
Over and over and over again.

Spreading our wings
And being nothing more.

In the end caterpillars liquify.
Cocoons wither into the dirt.
Butterflies fly free.

We are insects with wings,
being nothing more than what winged insects can be.

NOISE NOISE NOISE

But parallel lines never cross
and the screaming silence never stops.

Nothing ever is the way it seems,
and nothing seems the way it was.

Across the ringing plains;
noise noise noise noise
noise noise noise
noise.

Across the plains of Antarctica.

OIL

As the marquee
glows above you

the planes crash
into your head.

You use the flames
to light your cigarette.

The heat melts
your lipstick,
and paints your skin
a deep, deep red.

As the sun sets
we leave the lights out,
and use your head fire
to warm our toes.

WHEN WE WERE CHILDREN

The ringing in my head moved to
the tempo of the hole in the sky
and to the pace of the masses
flowing through the streets.

As the sky burst into flames.
As the sky collapsed to the ground.
As the walls of fire drew themselves inward.

Overwhelmed, I called out to you.

I can only pray that my voice drowned in the elements.
That it was not cast off for the cost of its weight.

I could see sweat glisten on your skin.
I saw the ocean in your eyes.

I watched ash rain onto the water.
Whales floating dead to the surface.

As a blanket of flame laid itself upon my body
I could see your arms trailing behind you

as you broke off my feet,
and threw me to the gods.

WHALES

Hear and see me
on the radio.

On your radio
and in the cold.

Hear the static
like a moan.

Hear the whales
through the phone.

Hear my voice
through the greying snow

and take it...

Know that I will always be
everything I need to be.

Know and see
I gained it all
the day life's
waves crashed
over me.

THE BACK WALL

She does her darndest
to push and pull and
moan and scream
and push some more
and gasp for air
and wonder where
there's room to spare.

Scootch and move
and feel down there
...
O dear god
no room to spare.

FAMILY PORTRAIT

So I knocked
the family portraits off the wall

along with newspaper clippings
from when my granddad was a kid.

The wooden frames
splintered on the floor,
and now we step on the glass.

I guess it's better this way,
I'm sort of glad that I did.

FALTAENIA

A large sip of bored brandy.
We're all so full of it, including yourself.
Left baby blue and faltaenic, I cannot get the taste of Ruth and salt out of my mouth. Plastered, dried, parched to the black and white sheets. Hot and dark, eating moths I cannot get enough of my own stink. Stuck to the cold and more so, soft, sour, steel. Chips and tea are all I eat, though it appears to shrink wrap me. Slowly, tighter, transparent and weak. Leaving a moist reservoir of dry grass dew, perception tears and pooled oil slew in the space by my collar bone. Brittle and crumbling. Not enough to feed the meek or pull the dry blood stitches out of the concave crevices inside my throat and cheeks. Though brilliant enough to match the shades and protect your eyes. Preparing to wrap my fingers in the strands of my own esophagus and musculature before I lose myself and spray noise.

The stitches pull out like thick cable, over thin steel.

Saturated, I slow down, catch myself and spray ecstasy through the air. A light mist of the common flea. Rat poison, putrid disposition. A light mist of the common fee. Plagiaristic, epidemic, forgettable and Teutonic.

Memorable because of the beauty it made, the death toll it took and the games it played with our children left them bleeding, speaking in lost and ancient Faltaenia. Sticking through blinding foreplay and laying on beds of nails propped against basement doors and brutally laid beyond recognition. Indescribable even by dim weak light perpetuated by my eyes and mouth acting as a coal miner's torch. Unable to penetrate the dark surrounded by old woods. At least burning their leather skin and letting me know how close they've come to perpendicular reconnaissance. Redemption, salvation, enlightenment, purity, self-preservation, blatant disregard for the synthetic order and the false belief in any spiritual isms. How close they've come to devouring me and their father through salivating osmosis. How close they've come to reflecting shattered distortions of a once beautiful mindscape and for once, possibly training themselves to be the only ones to ever live without it. I want to know how close they can come to becoming more than me, more than you, more then a mere deity, more than god. More than this world. I want to know how close they can come to becoming a universe in and of themselves. Totally devoid of all insecurities, inhibitions and dumbfoundings. I want to run my thin weak starved hands over the entirety of their clammy, sweaty, sticky, blood crusted seemingly lifeless bodies, and feel their heart pulse, and pulse, and pulse again, and then stop.

When my children's hearts stop, I want to throw my head back and burst my own ear drums with my laughter. I want to break a hole through the ceiling with the pride in my eyes and know that I created this life drained body that has now risen beyond any physical attributes. That this child of mine has become more than me or you or a mere deity or god. That this child of mine has reached for the lever to raise the nails up through the bed and reach a true omniscience.

No guilt for me to suckle out of the knots in their coffin's oak for through omniscience comes the deletion of time. Leaving it always, and the expansion of presence, leaving us everywhere. An accomplishment for an impeccable resume for a paradoxically perplexed time over matter, mathematic, infiltrating, kingdom collecting, out of body soaring, infantile minded and other wise mannered chemist.

Born of my own confidence. Though I am the shame I feel to my children. Empty of my worthiness, not enough to dig their place in the dirt or even give homage to the steel piercing flesh through this simultaneous mattress. Helped to comfort, true to feel, created to abort and with pain forcing us to deal. Reminded me in my youth the fundamental patronages and purposes to cutting my hair short, of always wearing gloves and keeping all appendages inside at all times. Away from trip wires and other shards of random objects I kept in cloth pockets that tore through leaving scars to later have tattoos of little secret numbers washed over them. After picking from the cobble stone streets in rain beaten parts of my joints. The flooded alleys of my palms and weathered valleys of rib and hip.

Shards of sharp that hung tied by frayed trip wires in place of shower curtains leaving room for black and white shirtless men, spiked jewelry, ragged pants. Blackened fingers suffocating in blacked out sightless gas masks tossed to the bottom of stained tubs and silently, violently, spraying blood lingering, disparaging vomit. Waist deep in a puddle of black and white slipping slowly down the drain trying to catch their breath. Gasping and choking like a three-year-old trying their hardest to cry as hard as they could. Their head soaked in sweat, tears, blood and bits of microwavable dinner, chunks of corn, balls of saliva and the partially digested mushrooms I did at four o'clock that morning.

When I'd finally caught my breath and taken control of the blinding pain the sweat in my eyes caused. Cleared the afterbirth from my throat and reoriented the blood flow through my arms. Pried the buckles and the blacked-out eyes of that gas mask from my head.

After I'd drunkenly pulled the sharp extremities from the curtain rod, and with handfuls washed my skin clean. After I'd smashed the mirror with my fists and painted my face a certain red. After I'd realized my eyes had changed color and had stopped dilating anymore at all. After I'd walked towards the camera watching me in black and washed over whiter tones. After I had reached for the red light beside the lens. After I'd slipped on puke and smashed my face through the linoleum floor, I saw into the hotel lobby.

I saw everything in full fucking color.
I saw my children on beds of nails.
I saw myself beaming with pride.
I saw me taping my reaction to it all
one frame at a time in a gray scale bathtub.
I saw me watch myself wash my face with broken glass.
I watched my pupils fail to focus.
I watched my pupils fail.
I watched myself watch me wallow in a gas mask.
I watched myself press record.

POSTMORTEM

We said we'd hang them
from the ceilings.

But now there's no them.

We used to say we'd do
a lot of things,
but we used to say a lot.

We used to have a god,
that we worshipped in
this worship building.

We used to say we'd get along.
But we used to say a lot.

TAROT

I will burn like god
and never ask for forgiveness.
I'll depend entirely on myself
and never bother with penance.
When I burn out it will happen,
in a matter of seconds.

And when they sweep up my body
my mother will thank
god I'm in heaven,
and never know,
I never asked for forgiveness.

At my funeral
my friends will wish
they had a stiff drink.
They'll pass out blue roses,
bow their heads in silence,
and say nothing.

www.ingramcontent.com/pod-product-compliance
Lightning Source LLC
Chambersburg PA
CBHW072135070526
44585CB00016B/1689